CUSTOM
SEMI TRUCKS 2

Bette S. Garber

First published in 2006 by MBI Publishing Company LLC and Crestline, an imprint of MBI Publishing Company, Galtier Plaza, Suite 200, 380 Jackson Street, St. Paul, MN 55101-3885 USA

The information in this book is true and complete to the best of our knowledge. All recommendations are made without any guarantee on the part of the author or Publisher, who also disclaim any liability incurred in connection with the use of this data or specific details.

We recognize, further, that some words, model names, and designations mentioned herein are the property of the trademark holder. We use them for identification purposes only. This is not an official publication.

MBI Publishing Company titles are also available at discounts in bulk quantity for industrial or sales-promotional use. For details write to Special Sales Manager at MBI Publishing Company, Galtier Plaza, Suite 200, 380 Jackson Street, St. Paul, MN 55101-3885 USA

Library of Congress Cataloging-in-Publication Data

Garber, Bette S.
  Custom semi trucks II / Bette S. Garber.
     p. cm.
  Includes index.
  ISBN-13: 978-0-7603-2714-2 (softbound)
  ISBN-10: 0-7603-2714-9 (softbound)
  1. Truck tractors—Customizing. 2. Tractor trailer combinations—Customizing. I. Title.
  TL230.5.T73G373 2006
  629.224—dc22
                                    2006019841

Editor: Amy Glaser
Designer: Kally Lane

Printed in Hong Kong

On the cover: An award-winning ride, *100HD* took first place in its class in its first show. Both the 22-inch front bumper and back T-bar are by Valley Chrome, and the headlights are custom-made. The tires are BFGoodrich 11x22.5s dressed with Alcoa-polished aluminum wheels. The 8-inch stacks wear Pickett elbows and donkey ear tops.

Inset: This Viper red Peterbilt 379 flamed with purple pearl doesn't show its 1,048,174 miles of road time. Note the louvered hood, flamed fenders, and the red touches on the wheels. Double JJ light bars accent the 22-inch bumper. The loaded 170-inch sleeper fills out a 358-inch wheelbase. With matching step-deck trailer, the combo sparkles with 396 lights and strobes. The truck carries four 100-gallon fuel tanks. The tires are BFGoodrich.

On the frontispiece: Painter Greg Stahl from Hampton, Minnesota, paints all of Eilen & Sons' trucks. He created these spectacular stylized flames for an Eilen daycab Peterbilt. The design is loosely based on the scimitar-edged tribal flame. Note the flames in the Peterbilt medallion.

On the title pages: Jimmy Hodge of Chattanooga, Tennessee, promotes positive awareness of the trucking industry with his 2006 Peterbilt 379X model tractor and 1989 Dorsey drop deck van that bears his personal credo, "Truckers are the Backbone of America." The patriotic artwork on all four sides was done by Phil Murphy of Rocky Face, Georgia.

On the back cover: The awesome front bumper carries a double row of clear-lensed LEDs, a whopping 108 inches, with the truck's name laser-cut into the bumper and backlit. Custom-painted murals and flames were done by Jay Griffin at the K & L Chrome Shop in Florence, South Carolina. Stainless toolboxes by Taylor Wing store their flatbed gear.

About the author
Bette S. Garber is the author of *Custom Semi Trucks* and *Custom Semi* and has been writing about and taking photos of semi trucks for over 25 years. She lives in Thorndale, Pennsylvania.

Contents

Introduction

Truckers like Billy Hopkins of Kaufman, Texas, tell me, "If you cut me open, trucks will come out." Mike McClane of Poplar Bluff, Missouri, who has family ties to trucking says, "I'm just kind of a truck fanatic in general."

It is truckers like these who create the awesome custom rides you will find inside this book. Some of the finest, most creative custom working trucks in North America, replete with visually stunning graphics and unique custom techniques, dazzling truck interiors, chromed and stainless engines, as well as brilliant arrays of exterior lighting, are featured within these pages.

I owe a big thank you to the many long haulers who were generous with their time and experience and to their families for extending help to me. Extra special thanks go to Bud Farquhar and Diana Owens of Stars & Stripes Events LLC.

This book offers a wider range of truck models than my first book, *Custom Semi Trucks*. Yes, the beautiful Peterbilts and handsome Kenworths are here, but so are more of the other truck makes that move freight across North America—Western Stars, Internationals, Freightliners, and even a Mack Vision and GMC. There are also more flatbeds, tankers, and specialty dumps, along with the dry van and reefer (refrigerated) trailers.

The fascinating, hardworking people who drive these unique custom rigs are at the heart of this book. You will meet many of them from all over the country. The trucks in this book were photographed predominately at truck shows, and for that reason they are spotless and meticulously detailed with no bugs, road dust, dirt, or grime to sully a grille. Tires, vinyl, and leather glow with protectant, and every piece of metal is polished to a jeweler's gleam.

Truckers roll into a truck show lot straight off the highway—dog-tired, yet ready and willing to put in the time to clean their rides to heights of trophy worthiness, including but not limited to lettering all tires, polishing all metal, waxing all paint, and making the interior spic 'n span.

What you need to know is this: owners of trucks this special are proud to the bone of their place in trucking and consider every day on the highway a truck show in and of itself. The trucks' appearance and maintenance are kept up, and they always look as good as time and weather will allow so that owners can collect the bouquets of compliments from an appreciative audience of peers. I consider my obvious bias for creatively enhanced semi trucks a badge of honor, and I am extremely proud of each and every truck on these pages.

Along with their noble rides, this book honors the truckers themselves for their artistry, dedication and pride in their profession. Now it is your turn to check out the scenery. Climb up into the driver's seat and discover the wonders of America's finest custom semi trucks.

Toweling off *The Beast*, Anthony Pesce of ETC readies his custom truck entry for competition. Believe it or not, this truck operated as an auto carrier before its amazing transformation. The 22-inch bumper comes to within an inch of the ground when the air is dropped. With the air bags inflated, it has 6 inches of clearance and 8 inches in the rear.

CHAPTER 1

Custom Semi Build-Off

Owner-operators intent on giving their truck a unique custom look either do the customizing themselves, or they seek out one of the go-to custom truck builders and chrome shops.

A rare breed, these specialists work on a large scale. They are familiar with trucks and what parts are best suited for customizing, and they know what looks good on a truck. Another important aspect is that they have the passion and imagination to create the elusive "something different" that takes a truck over the top.

At the 2005 Mid-America Trucking Show, five such maestros of metal and paint came together in a head-to-head competition in the first-ever Big Rig Build-Off.

An adjunct to the Stars and Stripes presentation of the Paul K. Young Memorial Truck Beauty Championships, the build-off attracted huge interest, drawing even more truck fans and media coverage to the already-popular working truck show.

The challenge was to take a no-holds-barred approach to building a truck, let creativity rule, and expense be damned. Entries did not have to be street legal or DOT certified.

The contest became a real test of their abilities and a challenge to show off what their considerable skills could conjure. The creativity that produced the build-off entries was clearly coming from a place where imagination was free to soar.

Distinctly different styles emerged, from classic to fantasy, each one attracting its own core of enthusiastic supporters. As wild as these trucks look, anyone seeing them cannot help but be inspired to consider the possibilities of transferring some of the creative concepts—the custom hoods, metal and fiberglass fabrication, paint—onto their own working rigs. Three of the five are featured here. Prepare to be inspired.

THE BEAST

ETC's Car Craft Truck Works
Staten Island, New York
www.elizabethtruckcenter.com

The powerhouse engine was completely overhauled and accented with stainless steel and chrome.

Declared Champion of the build-off, *The Beast* is a graphics-covered Candy Orange Peterbilt with Candy Apple Red frame and is the product of more than 8,000 man hours and four months of intense work by Anthony Pesce and his crew at Elizabeth Truck Center's Car Craft Truck Works facility in Staten Island, New York.

Pesce, 32, is a second-generation collision specialist with a passion for trucks. His family's companies,

Elizabeth Truck Center (ETC) and Car Craft Truck Works, have roots reaching back 30 years to the tough streets of Brooklyn, New York, where Pesce's dad, Steve Sr., and uncle John Pesce set up a heavy collision business that grew into sites in New Jersey and New York. Years later, Steve's sons, Steven and Anthony, joined them.

The Pesces opened a chrome shop four years ago to complement the collision business. ETC's Custom Chrome Shop has become a mecca for truck owners seeking cutting edge truck design and accessories.

(Left) *Pesce and his crew transformed the interior into a chromed and Ultrasueded palace equipped with elaborate surround sound and video systems. The luxurious seats swivel 360 degrees. Flooring is simulated granite with stainless trim.*

(Below) *Making a grand exit,* The Beast *offers a view of the magnificent custom rear light bar and over-the-top fiberglass fenders surrounding the wheels.*

In its previous life, The Beast was a wrecked 1999 Peterbilt 379 car carrier. Only the cab, engine, transmission, and rear suspension were salvaged. Pesce and his crew transformed it into a spectacularly customized champion on a 330-inch wheelbase.

"This was a monumental project," Pesce said, admitting the effort consumed him for months. "At 2 a.m. I'd wake up thinking about it and not fall asleep again. I'm glad people saw the truck for what it was. No detail was left untouched."

Pesce's concept was, in a word, overexaggerated from the long hood stretched 10 inches to Beast-worthy 10-inch stacks. "In a custom truck, people look for a low look, a long stretch, dropped visor, seats on the floor. We did all of that, but to the extreme," he explained. "In my mind it was a cartoon truck."

The Beast goes bright and bold in Imron 6000 custom Candy colors from duPont and intricate airbrushed graphics by Bill Streeter. Candy Orange on the body and Candy Apple Red on the frame were added in sheer, luminous layers for depth and brilliance.

Molded fiberglass front fenders drop 16 inches to wrap the tires. The front grille is custom billet aluminum. Custom dual headlights are Harley styled. The cab was chopped and required a custom windshield and visor. Suicide doors operate on remote electronics. The sleeper is chopped 8 inches.

Inside the orange Ultrasueded interior is a 12-speaker, 7,000-watt surround sound stereo. An elaborate video system projects onto a 27-inch plasma video screen in the rear with four 10-inch plasma screens mounted in the doors. Seats are customized Bostrom 360-degree swivel Low-Riders. Under the hood is a completely overhauled 550-horsepower Caterpillar 3406E with a custom cover over the manifold.

Pesce is understandably proud of the attention they paid to subtleties like matching up all the body lines and refinishing the dash to a perfectly smooth finish. The cab and sleeper were constructed to accommodate the heavy vibration of the sound system. "You can't see it, but the engineering is incredible," Pesce states with obvious pride.

All work was done at ETC's Car Craft Truck Works facility in Staten Island, New York. Members of the winning crew are Steve Pesce Sr., Steven Pesce Jr., Anthony Pesce, John Pesce, Angelo Mazzey, George Mazzey, Joe Mavica, Diego Mena, Gus Mena, Billy Kleber, Roger Conti, Wynton Telle, Bill Streeter, Mike Senerchia, Advanced Restoration, and Andrew Feltenstein.

MOBSLED

4 State Trucks, Inc.
Joplin, Missouri
www.4statetrucks.com
www.chromeshopmafia.com

MOBsled, the second-place finisher, is an all-curves lime green and white 1994 Freightliner Classic XL, constructed by Bryan Martin's creative team, "The Boyz," at 4 State Trucks in Joplin, Missouri. Popular with truckers all over the United States, 4 States is affectionately referred to as "the truckers' Wal-Mart" for its broad and deep selection of truck jewelry and parts. This talented crew literally exhales custom concepts—the same shop that built the now-famous bullet-riddled Outlaw truck.

The Boyz describe *MOBsled* as a "Hot rod Freight-Shaker raised from the wreckin' yard. The world's smoothest, lowest, baddest, loudest, sweetest, trickiest" 1994 Freightliner Classic XL on a 285-inch wheelbase. Its curvaceous custom hood is made by Truk-Rodz by Jones Performance.

The build was a collaborative effort with Pickett Custom Trucks in Marysville, Washington, owned by Rod and Kevin Pickett. In 2006, the two shops came together on *Trick My Truck*, a truck makeover television series seen on Country Music Television.

Martin described the two-way synergy between the shops. "We talked a lot and shared ideas. We have a similar look and style to our work. Pickett's

continued on page 16

Lime green and heavy chrome accents give this rebuilt Caterpillar engine attitude to spare. Note the absence of windshield wipers and exterior lights. A mere 10 inches of glass are visible below the visor.

(Above) *Meet* MOBsled, *4 State Trucks' mean, green, gangster machine. To truly appreciate the wealth of detail lavished on this so-called "hot rod Freight-Shaker," one needs to get above it for a birds-eye view.*

(Inset) *Inside details on this glorious gangster ride include dash panels sculpted in billet aluminum. The passenger door was suicided and the twin-stick tranny was topped with grenade handles. Also featured is a 5,600-watt Memphis sound system and three 7-inch television monitors.*

(Left) *Mean and low-down, that's* MOBsled *looking every bit the cool transport for bad boys who love bad toys. The custom airbrush artwork is by Ryan "Ryno" Templeton*

continued from page 12

is bare bone, simple paint, clean lines, long low wheelbase, 'lotta attitude' type trucks. We put a lot of that into *MOBsled*."

Clean is the basic theme—no rivets, straps, bolts, brackets. The truck is strictly for show, so there are no windshield wipers or exterior lights either. Color panels are punctuated with muraled accents, including a gorgeous babe painted on the rear frame cover. The cab is chopped 3 inches, leaving a squinting windshield with 10 inches of glass visible under the visor.

Inside is a stylishly curved billet aluminum dash and a twin-stick tranny. Its shifters are topped with green grenades. One wears a tag with instructions to pull pin and run when diesel fuel reaches $3 per gallon.

Projector contributors were Brunner's Fabrication, Truk-Rodz, Beatty Body Works, Ryan "Ryno" Templeton (airbrush), Rob Richardson, Valley Chrome Plating, Thunder Grafix Inc., Custom Billet, and Gailand Johnson.

SINGLED OUT

Quality Custom Inc.
Brampton, Ontario, Canada
www.qualitycustom.ca

Third place went to Brampton, Ontario's Quality Custom Inc., where owner Frank Fenwick, chief customizer Bruce Montgomery, and their staff went retro with *Singled Out*, an edgy 1930s-style 1983 Peterbilt 359 with flamed fenders and skull motif.

"We try to do things differently from everyone else," Montgomery says.

After removing 8 inches in front, chopping 6 inches in back, stretching the hood to 300 inches, and sloping the custom-grilled nose, *Singled Out* now resembles a low-slung hot rod roadster.

A snarling skull sets the mood on this roadster-inspired custom build. The superlong hood reaches out 300 inches and is finessed with flames. Note the long, graceful running boards that accent the 282-inch wheelbase

Skulls dominate as a design element. Base colors are Sunoco Blue and yellow. The dazzling airbrush paint was done by Kyle. Inside is hardwood flooring and a new Corvette-style dash with elaborate airbrush painting that repeats the skull theme. The doors are suicided.

Fiberglass front fenders appear to end in melted flames spilling onto the running boards. Under the wild hood is a 400-horsepower Caterpillar engine. The wheelbase is 282 inches, and the Goodyear Super Single tires were custom cut.

Singled Out is street legal in Canada. "It's not practical, but we can fully run all the trucks we build," Montgomery says. "This is just the beginning. Our goal is to be on a Discovery Channel–type show. We want to help dispel the negative image of trucks."

In September 2005 *Singled Out* was given away at a charity golf event benefiting Racing Against Drugs and Child Find of Ontario.

(Opposite) Deadman's curves give Quality Custom's Singled Out *its radical edge. The sinuous silhouette has few straight lines, but it has a lot of radical flames, cutouts, and drop-dead styling.*

(Below) On Singled Out *(left), custom fenders melt into flames, and more flames flicker down a length of highly polished stainless steel. The design is three-dimensional. Parked alongside* Singled Out *is another custom build from the same shop, a 2004 Peterbilt 379 on a 300-inch wheelbase that has already won its share of awards at Canadian competitions.*

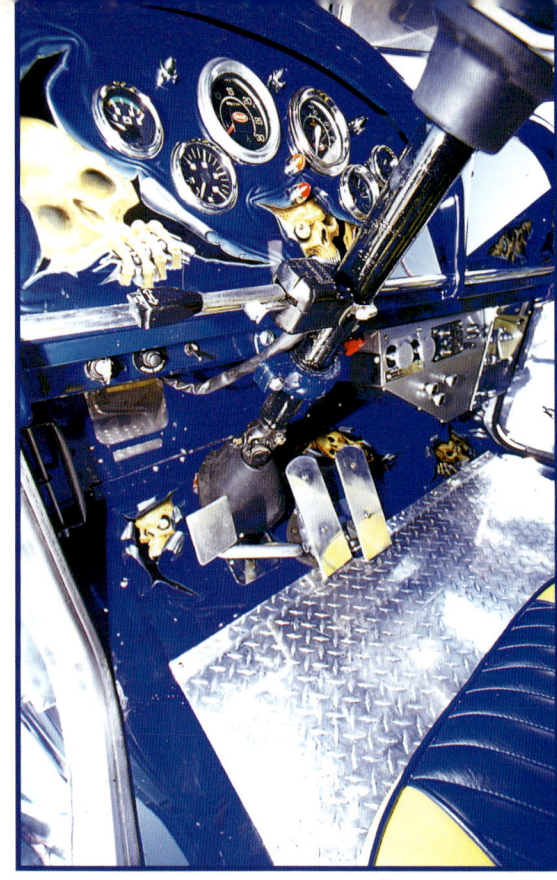

(Above) Airbrushed skullduggery reigns on a three-dimensional Corvette-style dash painted by Kyle. The skull motif is repeated throughout the interior. The floor is deck plate and hardwood.

An award-winning ride, 100HD took first place in its class in its first show. Both the 22-inch front bumper and back T-bar are by Valley Chrome, and the headlights are custom-made. The tires are BFGoodrich 11x22.5s dressed with Alcoa polished aluminum wheels. The 8-inch stacks wear Pickett elbows and donkey ear tops.

CHAPTER 2

Inspired By Harley-Davidson

Freedom-loving truckers love to ride motorcycles. These haulers need the sound and feel of power, much like a daily dose of vitamins, whether that jolt comes from kick-starting a bike to a deafening roar or releasing the muscle-packed thunder of diesel horsepower.

Call it the brotherhood of the white line: truckers who grind out mile after mile of grueling road duty and at the end of their run, climb down from their semis and mount a two-wheeled iron horse to ride off into another distant horizon.

Their motorcycling passion serves as an inspiration for how they customize trucks, with a clear bias toward the American-made Harley-Davidson. Harley stores are a popular shopping stop for shiny accessories that can be converted for truck use. Parts most commonly adapted to semis are head lamp visors, lights, and eagle-emblazoned tank badges. Foot pegs are also popular. Drivers mount them on either side of the pedals to add comfort to their ride.

When these motorcycle maniacs tap their inner creativity, they come up with applications like a Harley handlebar reconfigured into a fifth-wheel pin release or a grip that replaces a truck's steering wheel. Iowa trucker Ryan Avenarius created a unique hood ornament by mounting a Harley fuel tank cap badge to a piece of stainless and surrounding it with engine bolts.

Truckers bring their motorcycles with them on the road. Some create elaborate "garages" in a partitioned section of the sleeper box or mount the bikes to the truck's grille or deck. Sioux Falls, South Dakota, trucker Jim Heser mounts his 1982 Harley-Davidson Wide Glide onto the deck of the 1979 A-model extended hood Kenworth that pulls his Great Dane reefer spread axle trailer.

In this chapter, you will meet Oklahoma trucker Russ Brown, who mounted cut-down Harley handlebars on his Freightliner hood to serve double duty as both ornament and grip for tipping the hood.

On the exterior back wall of Brown's tractor is a copy of the famous David Mann painting titled "Brothers in the Wind." The interior of his cab and sleeper is 100 percent "Harley World," decorated in the signature colors of the Milwaukee-based brand. Even to the clothes he wears on the road, everything bears the Harley shield logo and colors.

Minnesotan Jake Eilen's Peterbilt, the other truck featured in this chapter, is similarly inspired by the Harley motif. From the flamed paint work to the eagle-muraled fifth-wheel cover, it displays Eilen's love for Harley bikes. "Live to drive, drive to live," a play on the popular biker's mantra, "live to ride, ride to live," is the legend sprawled across the back of Eilen's Harley-inspired tractor.

At least two truckers I know installed kickstands on their tractors…just for kicks, of course. To the Brothers in the Wind, this chapter is for you.

JAKE EILEN

Hampton, Minnesota
100HD
Tractor: 2003 Peterbilt 379
Wheelbase: 272 inches
Engine: one of a kind
Transmission: 18-speed; 3.55 rears

The eldest of three brothers growing up in a trucking family, Jake Eilen is an old hand at customizing trucks. He also loves to ride motorcycles, and his latest is a gorgeous Harley-Davidson 2004 Road King Custom. It's no surprise that Jake chose Harley-Davidson as the theme for his 2003 Peterbilt 379 extended hood. It captures the over-the-edge vibe of his motorcycle of choice.

Jake chose pearl black metallic as the dominant color. He wanted the frame to contrast, so he picked the orange accents. He asked painter Greg Stahl from Top Gun Kustoms to capture the Harley feel in the exterior paint. He wanted something wild, but not gaudy.

The result is pure, basic Harley flashed with custom-cut stainless steel, chrome, lights, and airbrushed flames. It's an eye magnet that instantly evokes the high-speed dreams of Jake's two-wheeler with its chrome-swept face and bold styling.

Jake named the truck *100HD* because he can't get out of a Harley store without spending more

A sleek stainless-steel box, fabricated in-house, is used during shows to cover up air lines, electrical cords, and hydraulic hoses. Note the tiny Peterbilt medallions tucked into nooks and crannies. No detail is too small for this trucking perfectionist.

than $100. He goes there for ideas, and he finds them on the shelves and in magazines and catalogs. "Then I make the parts fit the truck," he says.

Some examples are foot pedals he adapted and added to the throttle, brake pedal, and clutch in the truck. He installed cycle foot pegs on both sides of the pedal area as foot rests.

Jake and his brothers buy their own sheets of stainless steel and make most of the truck pieces in their shop. "Pretty much everything on this truck we made," Jake says, noting the Taylor Wing battery boxes and Brunner light bars under the doors as exceptions.

With a 36-inch bunk, this Harleyfied machine stands on a 272-inch wheelbase and pulls a variety of trailers: an end dump (sand, gravel, salt), tanker (liquid fertilizer), flatbed (machinery), and van (mail, freight). Harley attitude roars through the interior: seat belts, arm rests, a lacquered hardwood floor with an inlaid flamed "HD100", blankets, and pillows. He even converted a gas-pump-style globe light for the bunk.

The phrase "Drive to Live, Live to Ride" is painted across the back of the truck and has special meaning for this Hampton, Minnesota, trucker-biker. "You drive to make a living; you live to ride your motorcycle," he reasons.

This truck has been featured in two custom semi calendars.

Jake credits longtime family friend Mitch Larson and M & T Truck Repairs for helping keep the truck looking its best, and he thanks his wife, Anne, for all her understanding.

The stainless-steel plate was made at the Eilen & Sons' own shop and provides a gorgeous backdrop to display the Shell SuperRigs calendar shield. Note the Harley license plate on the tail end of the frame. The fifth wheel cover perfectly captures the Harley spirit.

RUSSELL AND DEBORAH BROWN

Oklahoma City, Oklahoma
American Thunder
Tractor: 1999 Freightliner
  Classic XL
Wheelbase: 264 inches
Engine: 430-horsepower Detroit
  Diesel Series 60
Transmission: 13-speed Eaton Fuller
overdrive; 2.90 Rockwell rear ratio

Growing up around motorcycles, Russ Brown didn't think it strange that the family vehicle was his dad's panhead Harley. He remembers, "We would use Grandpa's car if we needed one." A tricked-out 2001 Harley fatboy is now his ride of choice when he's not behind the wheel of American Thunder, which operates under lease to Mercer Transportation.

A long-haul trucker for 25 years, Russ has owned five tractors before this one, and two of them have been beautifully customized award-winning bobtails. This truck, purchased used in 2003, reflects his love for big-engined big iron of both the two-wheel and the 18-wheel variety. Its layers of detail—fearsome eagles, Harley-Davidson tank badges, black-and-orange paint—combine to make this truck scream "Harley bad ass."

American Thunder chases the wind across 120,000 miles annually, throughout the country, transporting military equipment on a step deck trailer.

American Thunder *mirrors the company colors of Harley-Davidson motorcycles. Square factory headlights have been replaced with two 7-inch round lamps by Double JJ in Anaheim, California. The area behind the headlamps is painted orange. Always-shiny Alcoa Dura-Bright wheels dress the 22.5 Firestone tires. Russ Brown installed the 130 Peterson LED lights with the help of Beatty Body Works. All of the stainless steel is by Rigskirts, including the custom grille.*

Harley medallions of all sizes decorate this interior, including the centerpiece on the steering wheel. Harley patches are sewn onto the door lining and onto new Talladega Low Rider seats by Bostrom. A saddlebag is mounted on the door for storage. There simply isn't enough room to list the wealth of H-D detailing in this truck.

The biker influence in this truck's design starts up front on the hood with chopped down motorcycle handlebars set with hand grips replacing the traditional hood ornament. The ornament base was made by Greg Schoenly. "People think it's pretty cool. And it's good for pulling the hood open," Brown says. The handlebar ornament draws so many compliments, Russ is already preparing to market his original design. In addition, Freightliner medallions were removed from the truck sides and replaced with tank badges from a 1957 Harley.

Russ and his wife, Debbie, have developed a reputation as skilled show-truck competitors.

Familiar design, new spin. Russ and Deborah Brown's names have been integrated into a Harley-style shield on the cab doors. Russ typically dresses in Harley garb from head to toe.

to owner-operator status and serious show competition.

Once a Swift Transportation line hauler, the truck was given a pearl white base coat swirled with purple pinstripes, but it lacked the snap and pop that Russ wanted. One day, heading eastbound out of an Iowa truck show, the Harley concept came to him. "I could see what it would look like and what I had to do."

The theme honors a painting by renowned biker-painter David Mann titled "Brothers in the Wind," which captures a high-ballin' 18-wheeler and a Harley rider thundering down the highway side-by-side. Those words are now emblazoned across the back of the truck sleeper. "Only bikers understand what it means," says Russ. "Some truckers ask me, 'Is that your brother's truck?' If I have to explain, they don't understand."

Working out of Beatty Body Works in Yukon, Oklahoma, Russ and Debbie, assisted by Chris Beatty and his staff, changed the paint to its current black and orange, added exterior art, tore down the motor, hiked the number of lights, and transformed the interior.

Their last two Kenworths, *Pure Attitude* and *Razor's Edge*, ruled national competitions for several years. The *Edge* was sold in 2002 when Russ opted to explore other employment opportunities in the industry. The desire to once again command his own custom ride eventually led him to acquire this Freightliner and return

The cabinet doors were built for the wall cubbies and painted a glossy orange and dressed with Harley tank badges. The sleeper's top bunk was removed, and in its place are shelves loaded with Harley knickknacks.

Pleased with the truck's transformation, Brown states matter-of-factly, "I may not be the first truck to [the] top of the hill, but I'm the best looking one when I get there." He grins, "I haven't figured out how to make the [430-horsepower] Detroit sound like a Harley yet, but give me time."

This Viper red Peterbilt 379 flamed with purple pearl doesn't show its 1,048,174 miles of road time. Note the louvered hood, flamed fenders, and the red touches on the wheels. Double JJ light bars accent the 22-inch bumper. The loaded 170-inch sleeper fills out a 358-inch wheelbase. With matching step-deck trailer, the combo sparkles with 396 lights and strobes. The truck carries four 100-gallon fuel tanks. The tires are BFGoodrich.

CHAPTER 3

Custom Profiles

TONEY AND DONNA BENNETT

Macks Creek, Missouri
Livin' Large
Tractor: 1999 Peterbilt 379
Wheelbase: 358 inches
Engine: 600-horsepower
  Caterpillar 3406E
Transmission: 18-speed; 3.08 rears
Trailer: Reinke 48-foot drop deck

Livin' Large can be called the ultimate truck. It's big, red, beautiful, loaded with the latest truck technology, and heavy on custom upgrades. Owners Toney and Donna Bennett drive together and average between 175,000 to 200,000 miles per year. Because of the truck's size and appearance, they are frequently asked if they also maintain a home. The answer is yes, but when they are delivering aircraft engines and parts to airports around the country, they prefer to stay in their truck in an atmosphere of their own making, and their choices are definitely heavy on comfort and style.

"Our main haul is aircraft engines. We haul anything that flies all over the U.S. for all the major airlines and equipment manufacturers," Toney explains. "We may have to sit overnight waiting for an engine at an airport. We can sit right there outside the client's door and have everything we need." The truck has operated under lease to Southern Pride in San Diego, California, for 11 years.

Livin' Large is 80 feet, 6 inches, long from bumper to bumper. "We mainly deliver to airports and manufacturing plants so we don't have to back up to docks or drive through construction," Toney says.

"We've always had nice trucks," he explains. "When we built this one, we took everything we'd seen and liked and added our own ideas. We're constantly doing something to it."

Wherever they go, they get noticed. "People come out of offices to look at it. They [have] never seen [a truck] so big and they want to know what's inside," Donna chimes in.

While not seen here, their red-framed 48-foot trailer is emblazoned with 150 lights. Of those lights, 146 are Truck-Lite LEDs with security bezels and four are Truck-Lite strobes. There are even strobe lights on the back of the trailer to ensure its visibility.

Other features include a built-in scale, electronic landing gear, and 10 ProTec side boxes. It also has auto wheel balancers, a tire-air equalizer system, and air ride with tractor bag adjustment.

Toney often offers words of caution to trucking newcomers who flock around his truck to ogle the flamed steps and spotlights, custom fenders, and shining steel.

"So many guys see the truck and don't realize how long it takes to get to a truck like this. We've worked hard to get to this point. This truck is six

This 170-inch Double Eagle sleeper is equipped with a 4-gallon water heater, a 60-gallon filtered-water storage system, a central vacuum, a shower-toilet, and a galley. Entertainment includes a TracVision in-motion satellite TV with 15-speaker Panasonic surround sound. Power comes from a three-cycle Kubota Gen-Pak 5.8kw diesel generator and a 1,500-watt Trace inverter/converter. The cab customization includes numerous stainless-steel, chrome, and rosewood accents, plus a 10-speaker Alpine AM/FM/XM/CD player with a 2,500-watt booster.

years old and it's paid for. Now we can make some real money. We don't know if there will be another one after this, but if there is, it will be as nice or nicer than this one."

Both owners drive and share 45 years of experience between them. "It helps a lot with her on the truck," says Toney, who has been driving for a total of 31 years, 17 of them solo.

"We're not always working, although we are on-call 24 hours out here. If we lay over, we sometimes rent a car and go sightseeing," says Donna, who stayed at home and worked in a bank while their daughter was in school. She planned for years to get onboard and has been behind the wheel with her husband for the past 14 years.

(Right) Everything is red on this truck—from the fender bras and mirror brackets to the steps, which are accented with purple pearl flames. Look into the stainless to see a reflection of the flamed fenders.

(Below) The mark of a truly great customized truck is in the details, such as the way the purple pearl flame motif is carried onto the Double JJ headlights. The same motif appears on the spotlights, stainless-steel steps, and fenders.

OWNER: MELVIN MAGGINI
DRIVER: MIKE MAGGINI

Maggini & Son Trucking
Riverdale, California
Pimpin' Ain't Easy
Tractor: 1998 Peterbilt 379
Wheelbase: 180 inches
Engine: 550-horsepower Caterpillar
3406E C15 Transmission: Super X;
  R170 rears
Trailer: 2002 Utility flatbed (semi
  and pull)

In the verdant farmland south of Fresno, California, family-run Maggini & Son Trucking rules the road. This radically flamed 1998 Peterbilt 379 and 2002 Utility flatbed set (semi and pull) combination is a superb example of the Maggini's distinctive fleet, but just about any of the trucks owned by the Maggini family are beautifully customized—a proud testimony to a business that's two, going on three, generations strong.

This multiple-award-winning ride is driven and was customized by Mike Maggini, the "son" in the company name. The combo transports 550 to 600 loads of hay annually to ranches and dairies throughout central California.

Pimpin' Ain't Easy demonstrates the heights to which a working truck can rise through imagination and creativity. Layer upon layer of detail includes stainless accents and pinstripes under the hood, plus a custom stainless firewall with the company name laser cut into it, and a red-hot

This 1998 Peterbilt 379 daycab has rolled over 460,000 miles. The old-style round headlights almost kiss the fenders. Why? "To be different. It looks better," Mike says. Paint is custom yellow zapped with candy green. Dale Lysdahl, the family's painter for 25 years, was killed in a motorcycle accident in 2004. He had painted all the Maggini trucks, motorcycles, cars, and pickups.

custom rear light bar on the trailer. All of the bolts are polished stainless steel. The driveline and U-bolts are chromed.

After dark, green neon glows like a carpet of fresh alfalfa under the tractor and trailers. Red lights under the frame add more accent. The family name shines green on the ground at night through a custom-cut stainless plate. "Kids love this truck," Mike Maggini says. "At truck shows they want you to autograph a picture. I get kids'

thumbs-up on the freeway. That's what makes it fun. The admiration is important. Must mean I'm doing something right."

In 1964, Mike's dad, Melvin, dropped out of high school to drive a truck, and Mike's uncle Felix joined Melvin. Today the elder Maggini owns 16 trucks, all Peterbilts. Felix owns four cabover Peterbilts. All bear the Maggini look of yellow kissed with candy green, and all the custom work is done in the company shop.

The 41 LEDs can't be missed on the custom rear light bar. It was made in the company's shop. The back sides of the 34-inch stainless fenders are painted black and pinstriped. Even the landing gear is elaborately customized with stainless steel, a shiny ace of spades welded on the side, and green lights on the inside of the column that backlight the company's name that is laser-cut into the steel.

A small sliding window was added to the back of the cab wall and framed with stainless steel. Through the window is a good view of the flamed airbrush work under the visor.

The entire family takes part in the daily operations of Maggini & Son. Mike's sisters run the office, with Annette taking care of commodities and hay and Barbara running the heavy-equipment hauling operations. One brother-in law, Bobby Ipsen, drives a 2000 Peterbilt, and the other, Bob Newsome, owns his own custom 2001 Peterbilt, which is leased to Maggini, of course. Uncle Felix buys and sells hay. Mike's wife, Jodi, leads the show team. Mom Jessie, whom I met when Mike's parents came to Las Vegas to see their son capture a Best of Show Bobtail trophy, is now essentially retired from managing the office and baby-sits her grandchildren full-time.

Besides hay, Maggini & Son Trucking transports large equipment, liquid fertilizer, and assorted commodities and produce using company-owned flatbeds, three walking floor trailers, two five-axle Murray low-bed trailers, one seven-axle trailer, two drop decks, a tanker, and a reefer.

CHARLES AND CAROL GRIMES

Sebree, Kentucky
Purple Passion
Tractor: 2000 Kenworth W900L
Wheelbase: 275 inches
Engine: 600-horsepower
  Caterpillar 3406E
Transmission: 18-speed; 3.55 rears

Charles and Carol Grimes' passion for purple is showcased in spectacular fashion on their ultraviolet pearl 2000 Kenworth W900L. Amazing lighting and airbrush work, white-and-lavender graphics, and custom stainless steel make this arguably one of the prettiest working trucks on the planet—and it looks equally good coming or going. The couple continually changes the truck's appearance, such as putting new spins on paint, lighting, and accessories to keep *Purple Passion* fresh, competitive, and jaw-droppingly beautiful.

Charles served in the Marine Corps for 20 years before he began trucking in 1970. At age 73, he continues to drive and pulls a reefer transporting aluminum from Henderson, Kentucky, to California, where he picks up fresh produce for the back haul.

The Grimes' have been married for 54 years, and their golden years leave them with no desire to enter multiple competitions. They compete every other year at one show. The venue they selected is the Paul K. Young Memorial Truck Beauty Championships presented by Stars and Stripes, LLC, which is held annually in Louisville, Kentucky, during the Mid-America Trucking Show. In every year that they have entered this event (2001, 2003, and 2005), the Grimes' swept

With its ultraviolet pearl paint glowing in the sun, Purple Passion wears a 22-inch Texas-style stainless-steel bumper dressed with 17 Panelite LED lights. Within the bumper, the truck's name is cut out and backlit with purple neon. A 12.5-inch louvered stainless drop visor shades the windshield. Vinyl graphics on the sides are by Auto Trim and Design of Middleton, Wisconsin. Tires are Goodyear 11Rx24.5-inch with Alcoa polished-aluminum wheels and Relative to Motion wheel covers.

(Above) Purple Passion *lights up gloriously at night with 144 Panelite LED lights and 16 tubes of purple neon. Note the raised rear frame cover that is customized with stainless steel.*

Best of Show honors. "*Purple Passion* came together just like we wanted it to," Carol says. "We've tried to keep it elegant, and not make it gaudy."

Their helpers at the show are their son Scott and his daughter Jacqueline. She likes to letter the tires. Jason Jones has been coming to the shows to help the Grimes since he was in high school. "He is the only person Charlie will let touch the stainless," Carol says. Purple floral arrangements in the truck's display are provided by Anita Leslie, a friend of Carol's.

The couple was surprised when the local newspaper, *The Sebree Banner,* ran a full-page story about the truck winning Best of Show honors.

(Left) *From the billet aluminum custom steering wheel with rosewood inserts to the marbleized dash, everything about this interior is customized. Note the chromed billet aluminum baseplate shifter and cup holders, and the lustrous rosewood panels on the glove box. The sleeper floor is shiny rosewood inlaid with the Grimes' name in script. The walls and closets are mirrored. All interior enhancements are from Rockwood Products.*

(Above left) *Stainless steel and chrome bring sparkle to the engine where even the manifold is stainless clad. The turbo compressor housing is painted ultraviolet pearl. Under the hood is a giant full-color graphic titled "The Mighty Cat," a jungle feline that the Grimes say is enormously popular with spectators. The engine was painted by Carol Grimes. Dave Gossman, the weekend service manager at the Kenworth garage in Evansville, Indiana, helped put the engine together.*

(Above right) Purple Passion's *proud owners, Charles and Carol Grimes.*

Everyone in Webster County, Kentucky, knows about *Purple Passion*. Its name and large photos of the couple, truck, and lavender engine were emblazoned across the top of the page.

At 72, Carol doesn't drive, but she has spent a lifetime helping her husband beautify his trucks. She does the detailing, is adept at shop work, and painted *Purple Passion's* engine lavender.

Their son Scott brags that his dad has a gift for creating beautiful trucks. "I get ideas from him. It's where he excels, putting things together, making things [on the truck] flow," he says. His mom agrees and adds, "He does have wonderful ideas."

Charlie hasn't missed a trick. He found stylish new wheel covers in Northridge, California, that no one else is showing. Bellagio covers by Relative to Motion add much to the truck's elegant appearance. They pop over the Alcoa polished-aluminum wheels like fine wheel jewelry.

A mural dominated by an eagle's head covers the back wall of the sleeper. Every detail has been carefully thought out and tastefully presented.

The interior, which was completely renovated in 2005, features mirrored walls, rosewood floors, and a marbleized dash. A rosewood plaque, backlit in purple neon, bears the name of the truck and takes up a large part of the sleeper's rear wall.

The couple's main sources for truck accessories and lights are Brunner's Fabrication, 4 State Trucks, Rockwood Products, and Relative to Motion.

DAVE BRANDT

Dave Brandt
Phoenix, Arizona
Eleanor
Tractor: 2003 Peterbilt 379
Wheelbase: 265 inches
Engine: 550-horsepower
  Caterpillar C15
Transmission: 13-speed; 3.55 rears

If looks could kill, this Peterbilt would be declared a lethal weapon. Startling images of writhing serpents; skulls; flames; and a fiery-tressed, shapely miss come together on Dave Brandt's 2003 Peterbilt 379 to offer an exotic visual experience not soon forgotten.

The custom artwork by Brent Speegle dominates three sides of the tractor, plus the hood. All art is executed in vinyl. Black pearl paint flecked with gold metallic is the broad canvas for the stunning imagery. Custom accents abound, further defining themes of life and death drawn from this trucker's wartime experiences in Vietnam.

Formerly a civil engineer, Brandt took to the road 16 years ago on the recommendation of a friend from the war and never regretted the decision. "I like the freedom," he says. "The variety of people you meet out here is amazing, from every walk of life."

The inspiration for the truck's way-out-there art direction came, interestingly, from a handful of stick-on tattoos purchased from a Laundromat vending machine. "They pointed me in the direction I wanted it to go," Brandt says.

The name "Eleanor" is laser-cut into the 18-inch stainless-steel Valley Chrome bumper. On the tractor are 153 clear LED lights by Trux Lighting, including 11 on the bumper. The skull motif is repeated in stainless steel on the hood and rear light bar, as well as inside the cab. The engine is equipped with a Gulf Coast foil filtering system. Pipes are Grand Rock 6-inch straights with "zero restriction" (no mufflers).

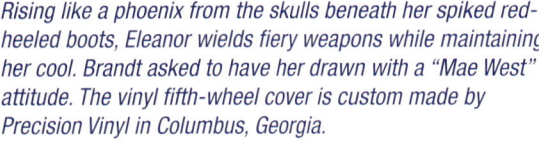

Rising like a phoenix from the skulls beneath her spiked red-heeled boots, Eleanor wields fiery weapons while maintaining her cool. Brandt asked to have her drawn with a "Mae West" attitude. The vinyl fifth-wheel cover is custom made by Precision Vinyl in Columbus, Georgia.

A U.S. Navy veteran and civil engineer by training, Dave Brandt changed professions 16 years ago and moved to over-the-road transport, where he has been a company driver, trainer, and owner-operator. The awesome imagery is the work of graphic artist Brent Speegle.

Airbrushed paint, a traditional choice for muraling trucks, was too expensive and would have cost $25,000 or more for the artwork Brandt envisioned, not to mention a possible month or more of downtime. So, he opted for vinyl. For $3,500 Brandt received his artwork, which was applied in a day and a half.

Vinyl art offers several significant benefits besides price. It's easy to remove and replace with relatively little expense or time, and its coloration remains brilliant without a clear coat.

Interior custom work includes chrome and stainless skull accents, rosewood trim on the doors and the headliner, a rosewood steering wheel, jeweled accents on the dash, and window cranks. Brandt also has an XM satellite radio, Sony tuner and receiver, and DX48T Galaxy CB radio. All interior enhancements were provided by Danny's Big Rig Truck Resort, in Phoenix, Arizona. "I want the shine to accent, not dominate," Brandt says.

Amenities include a built-in refrigerator, a microwave/convection oven, a 21-inch flat-screen color TV with VCR/DVD player and surround sound, and an enhanced closet with added shelves and storage.

Eleanor attracts attention wherever she goes. So much traffic stopped to gawk at Brandt's truck when he was unloading at a Sears store in Virginia that the police had to come and free up the road so the truck could get out.

Another time, Brandt parked outside a desert motel, went in, then realized that he forgot something and had to go back to the truck. He found a crowd of European tourists gathered around it, taking pictures. Retrieving the item he needed, he tapped on the train whistle as he exited. The startled onlookers applauded. "I took off my hat and bowed. It was great." He currently pulls a dry van hauling general freight under lease to Schneider National.

This totally extreme rear light bar is stainless steel, as are all the light bars under the sleeper, cab, and tool boxes. The skulls are from the Chrome Oasis in Danny's Big Rig Truck Resort in Phoenix, Arizona.

JOHN AND AMY HOLMGREN

Shafer, Minnesota
The Rolling Memorial
Tractor: 1999 Freightliner Century
Wheelbase: 247 inches
Engine: 550-horsepower
  Caterpillar
Transmission: 10-speed
Trailer: 53-foot 2001 Utility

In 2002, John and Amy Holmgren, over-the-road truckers for more than 20 years, decided to transform their present tractor-trailer into a rolling memorial to the heroes and victims of the events of September 11, 2001. A song by country artist Darryl Worley, "Have You Forgotten?" inspired the Holmgrens and pointed the way to this truck's theme and graphics.

Their previous truck had featured a small 9/11 memorial mural. "People took notice. That started us thinking about creating a special truck that was one entire tribute to the fallen," John explains. *Have You Forgotten?* is the name they gave their truck, but it has come to be known as *The Rolling Memorial.*

The names of all police officers, fire-fighters, EMTs, port authority officials, and search dogs who died in the attack are saluted as heroes on the tractor. On the trailer, 3,100 names of people who perished in the World Trade Center Twin Towers, the Pentagon, and the four airplanes have been memorialized and integrated into the overall design with spare but emotionally inspired graphics.

Photographed by the Allegheny River in Kittanning, Pennsylvania, The Rolling Memorial displays Kosienski's hand-painted tractor artwork, including a two-piece continuous mural on the hood and roof that honors New York City fire-fighters as they raise the U.S. flag at Ground Zero.

The artwork on the rear doors honors the victims of the 9/11 attack on the Pentagon. The 4x8-foot scrolls, two on each side, list the names of flight crews, pilots, and passengers killed on the four airplanes, as well as names of those who died in the World Trade Center. Artwork is by Paul Kosienski of Whiplash Signs in Fargo, North Dakota; Arlee Simpson from Applied Images, LLC; and Ryan Kava, a graphic designer.

The center mural on The Rolling Memorial's *trailer has 18 columns of victims who died in the Twin Towers, with 85 names per column.*

This truck has been creating qutie a buzz, thanks to a e-mail sent in early 2004. John believes its source was someone at a food company in Sterling, Illinois, who photographed the truck as the couple was unloading produce. The e-mail appeared to take on a life of its own, wriggling into corners of America and causing recipients to take notice and keep forwarding it on.

As the e-mails continued to build interest, requests for appearances followed. Famous entertainers such as Lee Greenwood, Reba McEntire, Jimmy Buffet, and Darryl Worley received the e-mail and asked the Holmgrens to bring the truck to their concerts.

The Rolling Memorial was present at the commemorative ceremony held at Ground Zero in 2004 and is currently featured on 37 websites. There is even a 1:64 metal diecast model available on the Holmgrens' website, www.therollingmemorial.com.

Make no mistake, the Holmgrens are ordinary truckers and self-described "average working stiffs" with a combined 4.5 million accident-free miles under their seat belts. Operating as Rosepath Transportation, the couple transports Roman Meal products west and brings produce back east. They work closely with their carrier to route pickups and deliveries to coincide with their appearances. For now they continue to deliver freight while bringing *The Rolling Memorial* to Americans throughout the country.

The Holmgrens have created something extraordinary, and the world is taking notice in ways that leave these unassuming folks shaking their heads in amazement. When people see the truck, they surge toward it as if pulled by a magnet, falling silent to solemnly contemplate all the names. "We can park this anywhere and within five minutes we'll have someone knocking on the door asking to take photos," says John. "We started out with nothing and almost lost it all along the way. If not for the Lord and our friends, we couldn't have done this."

THOMAS AND KIMBERLY TURNER

Cynthiana, Kentucky
El Dorado
Tractor: 1995 Peterbilt 379
Wheelbase: 324 inches
Engine: 550-horsepower
   Caterpillar 3406E
Transmission: 13-speed; 3.07 rears
Trailer: 2003 Transcraft step deck

Unlike the legendary lost city of gold, the namesake of this teakwood-and-beige combo, *El Dorado* brings its owners bonafide riches measured in happiness, fulfillment, and hard-earned pride in their awesome ride. Unique approaches to chrome, lighting, and custom stainless set this truck apart and clearly reflect the attention paid by the owners to making their truck live up to its potential.

This is Tom and Kim's second truck, and it's an award-winner that hauls multimillion dollar aviation equipment to airports all over America. Living their dream in a dream truck, the Turners say, "We've found our El Dorado in this truck. That's why its accent color is gold." The engine and pinstripes have been painted gold and many of the details are trimmed with 18-karat gold leaf.

The truck boasts chromed shocks detailed with gold leaf; tooled leather-looking vinyl covers on the engine, fenders, and cabinet doors; plus silver-buckle door knobs and bullet-casing toggle switches with sparkling jewels on the custom dash. The custom-designed truck medallions glitter with gold leaf. Even the landing gear is customized with

El Dorado is a handsome combination of teakwood and beige with opulent gold leaf accents, more than 500 Maxxima LED lights, plus lots of chromed and custom stainless pieces. Light bars down the side of the trailer are stainless Western trailer brackets. Note the custom nosepiece on the hood, the chromed fender guards, and the tooled leather-looking vinyl fender bras.

48

boilerplate steel dolly pads in the shape of wagon wheels. A whopping 12 stainless-steel boxes on the trailer hold all the straps, specialty tarps, and chains. Wood support pieces have a compartment of their own with a stainless-steel door. Every inch of this ride reflects the same careful attention to detail.

Tom, 50, has been driving professionally, off and on, for 28 years. He has alternated between farming and trucking, and early on he started hauling his own grain and soybeans. In 1996, he joined Crete Carriers as a company driver, and three years later he purchased a new Freightliner truck through the company. He dressed it up with 400-plus lights and special custom details. Tom acquired this truck used in 2004 and he is its third owner. The trailer was repainted and relit, and many details were added to accentuate the Western motif.

For many years Kim, 34, rode along and kept Tom company, but after they bought the first truck, she acquired her CDL. "There was no sense just riding along when it was our own truck," she reasons. Now leased to Southern Pride, the couple feels like they have struck proverbial gold. "You can always tell a Southern Pride truck from the big bunks, and we always wanted to get involved with them."

At *El Dorado's* debut competition, the Paul K. Young Memorial Truck Beauty Championships presented by Stars and Stripes, LLC, the combo was voted Best of Show. It repeated its performance the following month at the North American Trucking Show and earned the top spot.

"Tom always wanted something good enough to bring to Louisville. It's the biggest, hardest show to win, so we worked to that point. We just decided to go for it," Kim says. Tom's daughter-in-law, Jessica, helped them with the polishing and presentation.

A painted plaque on the passenger side of the truck honors the memory of the couple's longtime friendship with Billy Sones, a fellow driver they met while at Crete. "He would get so excited when we talked about a show truck!" Kim says. "It was a one-of-a-kind friendship that you don't find that often. He and his wife were family to us."

It's unusual to see a cab go for a light look in paint and appointments. This one is sensational and has an ivory-colored steering wheel and bullet casings of various sizes fashioned into switch handles. Kim added jewels to the primer holes. Red LED rope lighting gives the area even more drama. The dash was custom built for the truck by Rockwood Products. Much of the detail work was performed by Truk-Rodz/Peterbilt of Joplin.

Painted gold metallic with shimmers of pearl, the 550-horsepower Caterpillar 3406E engine is a showpiece and is embellished with shotgun-shell endcaps and chrome, gold leaf, and leather-like tooled vinyl wraps on the manifold.

Leather-like tooled vinyl covers the full deck and adds a Western style on fenders and tool boxes.

RUSTY WYRICK AND TINA LOMAX

Mansfield, Ohio
French Quarters
Tractor: 1998 Western Star Constellation
Wheelbase: 325 inches
Engine: 500-horsepower Detroit Diesel Series 60
Transmission: 15-speed Eaton
   Fuller overdrive

The good-time spirit of Mardi Gras revelry in New Orleans is translated here in Rusty Wyrick and Tina Lomax's *French Quarters*, a festively appointed Western Star with a 150-inch ICT sleeper. Its theme pays homage to the Queen City's annual pre-Lenten free-for-all party. Obvious glamour aside, it is a working truck specializing in executive relocation throughout the United States. Between April and November, *French Quarters* transports 250,000 pounds of household goods, about 25,000 pounds of furniture and boxes per load, averaging between 1,000 to 1,200 pieces per shipment. It's stored for the winter, and a swing truck takes over during the bad weather months.

A spectacular sight both inside and out, the truck makes an indelible impression as it pulls up to a customer's residence pulling a 51-foot specialty moving van. "My customers light up when they see the truck," Wyrick says. "I can almost hear them thinking, 'If he takes care of the truck like that. . . .' My entire team is in uniform, dressed professionally. People know they are in good hands."

Like the Mardi Gras parades that light up the French Quarter, this truck is a rolling light show with 1,142 LEDs and neon bars. The bumper features 18 neon bars in purple, green, and red-orange; nine 6-inch LEDs; plus tragedy/comedy masks laser-cut from polished stainless steel. The mask theme also appears on the custom hub rockers on the wheels and at various places around the truck. Technical assistance was provided by Tim Arthur.

53

An arresting portrait of a devilishly droll jester covers the hood. Much of the elaborate detail for which this truck is famous can be seen here, including the laser-cut bumper, stained-glass window, and the tragedy/comedy mask motif. Note the jester hats capping the stacks.

Wyrick has put in some serious research time on this project. The truck's wealth of detail is, like the spirit of Mardi Gras, often over the top. There are 1,142 lights, both neon and LEDs, which are enough to light a parade all by themselves. There are also several stained-glass windows and Tiffany-style glass sconces and shades; bright red leather cab upholstery; a three-dimensional carved tabletop, hand-painted and under glass, that depicts a street scene in the French Quarter.

The exterior murals on both sides of the bunk were painted by brothers Dave and Al Thomas from Edmonton, Alberta, and feature well-known New Orleans landmarks such as the street celebrations and parades, and even the city's legendary voodoo queen, Marie Leveaux. On the hood is a striking portrait of a macabre Jester with a mouthful of demon teeth. "I wanted something for everybody; something serious, happy, even scary," Wyrick explains.

An energetic buzzsaw of a man, Wyrick received his CDL in Dallas, Texas, at age 25 and took a job moving furniture. He enjoyed helping people move and made it his life's work. Eventually he became

Under the hood, the 500-horsepower Detroit Diesel Series 60 is as elaborately decorated as a Mardi Gras king cake in symbolic colors: green for faith, purple for justice, and gold for power.

The centerpiece to the elegant dining area is a hand-carved cherrywood tabletop by Ohio artist Donna Grantham, who created a three-dimensional view of the French Quarter with fireworks lighting up the background. Multicolor glass globes cover the lights on walls and ceiling, adding to the luxurious atmosphere. All of the chairs in the dinette and cab are upholstered in red leather. The cabinets and flooring are made from cherrywood; the ceiling is mirrored; plus the full kitchen, bathroom, and four closets are inset with stained glass.

an owner-operator. *French Quarters* is his fourth and final truck.

Wyrick operates under lease to Palmer Moving and Storage in the North American Van Lines system in the Executive Relocation Division. The proud recipient of numerous service awards and one of Palmer's top-10 operators for quality service, Wyrick generously shares the credit with his team, which besides him and Tina includes two permanent helpers, Tom O'Leary and Matt Martin. "Your quality is only as good as your crew. We're like an oiled machine," he says. "Tina is my pad queen, and I do the actual loading myself." He proudly explains, "We do it right. Sometimes it takes all four of us to prep the house. It's all about professionalism."

French Quarters competes at many popular truck shows and is a frequent trophy winner. The couple works together to clean and prep the truck. As a final accent, they even sprinkle glitter on the ground in the Mardi Gras traditional colors of purple, green, and gold. After 20 years of moving households, "I've proved myself," Wyrick says. "I finally made it to the 'big dogs' [Executive Relocation Division], and I have the truck of my dreams."

EILEN & SONS TRUCKING

STREET PETE

Tractor: 1988 Peterbilt 379
extended hood
Wheelbase: 250 inches
Engine: 700-horsepower Cummins
Transmission: 15-speed; 3.36 rears
Trailer: 50-foot 1994 Featherlite

NITRO BUCKET

Tractor: 2003 Peterbilt 379
  extended hood
Wheelbase: 300 inches
Engine: 450-horsepower
  Caterpillar C12
Transmission: Allison automatic;
  4.88 rears
Trailer: 21-foot MAC dump body

LET'S RIDE

Tractor: 2003 Peterbilt 379
  extended hood
Wheelbase: 270 inches
Engine: 550-horsepower
  Caterpillar C15
Transmission: 18-speed; 3.55 rears
Trailer: 2003 MAC end dump

This outrageous combo transports Jonathan Eilen's asphalt late-model race car. Flames painted by Greg Stahl scorch the trailer, which hauled Terry Labonte's championship car. The combo shines with 115 lights. This truck has over a million miles on it and a killer engine to boot. "It definitely gets us to the racetrack and back pretty quick," says Eilen. Custom enhancements include racing-style hood pins, a spoiler on the back of the sleeper, and Grand General 7-inch stacks with turnouts. Inside, there's a helmet hook!

At Eilen & Sons Trucking, Tom Eilen still specs all his equipment, but his sons, Jake (24), Pat (22), and Jonathan (20), now design the trucks and give a whole new look to the family business. The working semis these young men customize are winning loads of trophies, appearing in prestigious industry calendars, and collecting compliments wherever they go.

Four of the family's trucks compete at shows. The three seen here are owned by the company. Jake owns two trucks, but competes with only one—a black Peterbilt 379 he calls *100HD*. (See Chapter 2, Inspired by Harley-Davidson.)

Tom started the business in 1972 and bought his first semi 6 months after he graduated from high school. He now owns 30.

Their dad remembers his childrens' fierce interest in show trucks. On a southbound family trip, he recalls how the boys spotted Canadian

(Above) *Tom Eilen's youngsters (left to right: Jake, Jonathan, and Pat) grew up to become truckers with unique customization techniques all their own. All the boys drive and design trucks.*

(Below) Nitro Bucket *rules the night with over 250 lights—an extreme combination of clear American SuperLites, strobes, and neon.*

Billy Baker's well-known show truck at a truck stop. "They made me turn around and go back to see it," Tom recounts. "They picked up right away on the truck's eight-bolt hubs."

Tom matter-of-factly acknowledges his sons' intuitive skills for customizing. In fact, the boys now design their semi creations under the name EAST Customs. EAST is an acronym for Eilen & Sons Trucking. "They want to build [trucks] differently than everyone else. That is their motive," their proud father relates.

The painter behind the flaming designs is Greg Stahl from Top Gun Kustoms. BT Design did the company lettering, the Father Time cartoon, and the unit number. Stainless-steel items such as the smooth deck plate, light bars, and drop visors were made in the Eilens' shop with the help of Mark Mathees and Keith Hubbard.

(Below) Asphalt, sand, and gravel take a wild ride in Nitro Bucket. *This truck sports a silver metallic and medium-blue metallic frame and red-hot flames. The truck's driver, Pat Eilen, did the custom work. The custom-ordered 22-inch Valley Chrome bumper is slightly tapered and has a frenched-in license-plate holder. Note the Kenworth grille bars, Double JJ headlights, and turn signals. The truck has undergone lots of changes since this photo was taken, but Pat makes sure it always looks awesome.*

Pat Eilen helps letter the tires on Let's Ride. *An array of clean, polished, and lettered tires speaks volumes to judges about the effort spent preparing a truck for show.*

Bursting with the juicy goodness of citrus colors and custom details, this striking tractor is combined with a super-shiny 2003 MAC end dump trailer. Airbrushed flames fire up not just the hood, but the front and rear fenders as well. Custom touches include a 22-inch chrome bumper with custom-tapered corners by Valley Chrome. Double JJ light brackets, light bars down both sides, and 195 lights add even more glamour.

HARVEY AND KAREN ZANDER

St. Louis Park, Minnesota
Icy Blu 2
Tractor: 2003 International 9900ix
Wheelbase: 264 inches
Engine: ISX 600 Cummins
Transmission: 18-speed auto-shift;
   3.73 rears

Harvey Zander and his wife, Karen, epitomize the gold standard in trucking. Besides owning and operating this show-stopping ride, the couple is actively engaged in promoting driver safety and a positive trucker image through extracurricular activities such as teaching road safety to high school students and corresponding with a fourth-grade class through the Trucker Buddy pen-pal program.

These attributes helped Zander become the only trucker ever to have twice won the Truckload Carriers Association's Independent Contractor of the Year award (1990 and 2000). And with those honors, he won two trucks. *Icy Blu 2* is the truck he won in 2000 and it now shows 236,938 miles on the odometer. The truck's name and theme are tied to the seascape blue color that suggests a winter sky in Minnesota. Snow and ice play a major role in the murals and decor, as do family images.

Since 1970, Zander has been plying the highways, and for the past 25 years he has been under lease to Dart Transit. He will soon celebrate 4 million safe miles of driving. "It doesn't hurt to slow down," he says.

The seascape blue base color on Icy Blu 2 *evokes the frigid winter skies of northern Minnesota. The integral sleeper is a 72-inch High Rise. Valley Chrome Plating made the 20-inch front and back bumpers. Both pieces are custom made and laser-cut with the truck's name and backlit with LED lights. Alcoa's Dura-Bright wheels, setting off the 11x22.5 full-size Goodyear rubber, have a nonstop shine that never needs polishing.*

On the bunk's driver's side, the couple's grandson, Jake, makes trucks in the snow representing Zander's past trucks. Footprints from the German shepherd (background) patter down the rear left fender. At the top rear, an angel honors the memory of Harvey's child, Tatum Rae. On the map below, vacation spots the Zanders have visited together in the truck are pinpointed.

Zander is currently operating within a Dart dedicated fleet for Silgan Container Corporation and hauls tin plates for food cans and lids. "Lids are heavy," he says, noting the weight of a lid load is about 42,250 pounds. How many lids make up this heavy load? As many as two million!

Like so many truckers, Zander grew up in trucking and helped his dad haul milk in cans from farmers' yards. "I was always in the truck with him when I wasn't in school or church," he shares. After a stint in military service, Zander became a full-time hauler.

Zander's wife does not share driving duties, but Karen plays a central role in the couple's business and outreach activities, and she also brings considerable creative talents to designing and improving their trucks. "She keeps coming up with endless things to do. Get out of the way until she gets it done," says her husband. "I never would have won the TCA [competition] without her."

Visually the tractor dazzles with 300 LED lights by Truck-Lite. By night it skates on an icy slick of Street Glow blue neon. Most of the custom stainless-steel pieces were done by Roadworks. The pieces on the back fairings, deck plate, and engine are by Eddie Watson. D & S Plating did the custom chrome, including the alternator case and door controls. "Chrome is so much easier to take care of," Zander insists. "Just wipe it with a damp cloth. It will shine."

Icy Blu 2 is a treasure trove of creative customizing ideas that improve and enhance all aspects of the bobtail, inside and out. The interior was gutted, and a computer analysis determined how to best use the space. "We wanted to use every inch," Karen says. Michigan carpenter Bob Foster built the oak cabinets, headliner, and a console that houses the Qualcomm unit, satellite radio, eight-disc CD changer, and cassette player. The console top comes off with four screws for easy access. Loads of chrome plastic from Lifetime dress the dash. Chrome extensions tipped in blue jewels and the rosewood-and-chrome steering wheel are from Woody's. The Comfort-Ride seats sit on

Six cabinet doors feature infinity lights that appear to go on forever. The effect is achieved by making a hole in the doors, adding Plexiglas and lights, followed by a mirror. During the day, only the mirror is seen. A pullout stainless sink with running water (10-gallon reservoir) was added. Several drawers were also built, including a large one under the bunk. Amenities include satellite TV, refrigerator, and microwave.

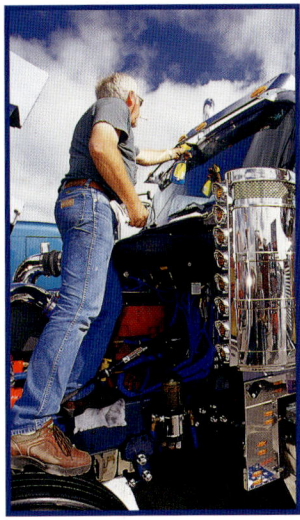

Much of the engine is dressed with chrome and stainless. All of the brackets, bars, and steering arms are chromed, as are the pedals for clutch, brake, and accelerator. "The chrome brackets set off the color of the engine," Zander says. Karen recently painted the engine herself in GM metallic red. "She painted it by brush, and you won't find a brush stroke on it," her husband notes.

custom oak bases. The shifter knob is also custom made from oak. Instant on-off lights illuminate all the cabinets. "It's easy to do, like a glove-box light," Karen says. "These are great at night. I love 'em." The refrigerator was raised off the floor, which makes it easier to access. "Now Harvey can reach behind his seat to get a drink," Karen says. Additionally, storage space was created underneath.

Cork flooring—arguably the first in a truck—has excellent insulating properties that keep warmth in and sounds at a minimum, the couple says. "We didn't want plain wood. Everyone has that," Karen explains. "Cork is easy to cut and cushiony. If you drop something on it, it dents, but comes back. Scratches can be sanded out and refinished."

A half-inch raised lip edge was added to the counter surfaces and cabinet openings. "A smooth countertop won't take you two miles down the road," she notes. The bunk quilt, curtains, and most of the fabric pieces are all her handiwork.

Standout murals cover three exterior sides. In addition, snowy drifts and icicles are painted on most surfaces. The airbrushed paint is by Art Rig's Jim Shively.

The couple's grandchildren, Rebecca and Jake, are featured on the side murals. On the sleeper's back, a haloed angel is a tribute to Tatum Rae, nicknamed "T," Harvey's daughter with his first wife. Tatum succumbed to a respiratory infection at 17 months over 30 years ago. The couple's company name, "T-RaCo" honors her as well. "When you lose a loved one, there isn't a day that goes by that you don't think about her. This way she is with me all the time," Zander volunteers. "You wonder what she'd be like. It goes through your mind every day."

RICK ROLLMAN

Lititz, Pennsylvania
Tractor: 2002 Peterbilt 379
    extended hood
Wheelbase: 270 inches
Engine: 550-horsepower
    Caterpillar 3406E
Transmission: 18-speed; 3.55 rears

The Rollman family has been hauling freight out of Lititz, Pennsylvania, for almost 100 years. Joshua Rollman started the business in 1918 using a horse team and dray wagon to transport local goods to the Lititz railroad freight station. His business became known as J. Rollman and Sons, Inc. Today his great-grandson Rick Rollman, 47, carries on the family tradition and operates his own truck. He began his driving career at 17 and ran between Philadelphia and Pittsburgh. Several of his present-day customers are the same companies that Joshua served many decades ago.

That Rick's love for trucks and customizing is born of some genetic predisposition to the craft becomes apparent when looking closely at the detail work on his distinctive white Peterbilt slashed with purple tribal-style flames. The look he favors for his Peterbilt is heavy on highly polished metal with accents coming from extraordinary airbrushed flames. His lighting choice is clear-lensed LEDs by American SuperLite that blend right into the white silhouette during the day. It's a deliberate choice to keep the emphasis on the awesome metal. At night, six tubes of purple neon reflect wildly off all the shiny sur-

Rollman's Imron 6000 white Peterbilt accented with casino purple stands tall with twin straight pipes mounted with stainless exhaust brackets. Visor is by Rigskirts. Oval Vortox air cleaners are mounted without straps and add to the clean profile. The WTI rear fenders are shadow flamed by Dan. The stainless rear light panel is customized with six LEDs, and the steps are polished aluminum. One-inch stainless trim, without lights, adds shine to the cab and bunk.

Under the hood and fenders everything shines. The inside of the hood, fenders, and firewall are all completely lined in stainless. Rollman painted the engine white, and the valve covers are purple with stainless inserts. Shocks, steering shaft, spring covers, filter wraps, and the radiator tank cover are stainless. The shine continues with a polished-aluminum turbo housing and chrome-plated water and air-intake pipes.

faces. "I wanted to give it the old hot rod look with flames. People's reaction to the truck is always positive and they give me the thumbs-up," says Rollman, who has been around trucks his entire life. "I just like trucks. I enjoy working on mine and showing it off."

Rollman's custom-designed truck has won countless trophies and honors. When it isn't competing for bragging rights, it hauls pet-care and chocolate products made in Lititz, then back hauls raw materials to the same plants. The truck has rolled across 350,000 miles that cover all states east of the Mississippi.

All of the work on the truck was done by Rollman and his friends in his own garage. Custom fabricated

A fanatic for clean and uncomplicated trim, Rollman mounted stainless strips to cover the bolt heads on the frame. He got the idea in a last-minute burst of creativity prior to a truck show.

Rollman's interior resembles a house of mirrors. The bunk is surrounded by mirror-polished stainless steel and lit with purple neon. The floor is purple-and-white vinyl tile. Wood trim adds warmth to the highly metallic interior that features a stainless shift-plate cover, side strips, seat bases, and even a custom stainless drink cup holder. The overhead console holding the radio is also stainless. The chrome shifter knob is by Whelan Brothers.

stainless pieces were fashioned by ProFab Associates in nearby Manheim and installed personally by Rollman and his crew. Among some of the more notable pieces are stainless-covered rear springs, air bag saddle, and even the top of the air bags. The entire deck and frame, which is 8 feet long, are wrapped in stainless. Few trucks can match the high level of customization on Rollman's truck, but then, trucking's been in his genes for four generations and has given him the talent to create this truck's unique custom look.

LARRY AND TAMMY WINKLER

Grandview, Indiana
Barnyard Beast
Tractor: 1985 Peterbilt 359 extended hood
Wheelbase: 315 inches
  (63-inch flattop sleeper)
Engine: 450-horsepower
  Peterbilt 3406B
Transmission: 15-speed OD Fuller; 3.90 rears

A trucker since 1979, Larry Winkler bought this Peterbilt with a 63-inch flattop sleeper from its original owner in 1990. Winkler drove the truck for 10 years and hauled farm machinery on a 48-foot drop deck. He quit the road in 2000 and opened a truck detail shop and trailer resale business in southern Indiana. *Barnyard Beast* was totally rebuilt to crouch low to the ground and was painted and polished out. Winkler and his wife, Tammy, did most of the work themselves.

The interior is restyled in flame-embossed tweed by Gwenmar Upholstery and the owner's own hardwood flooring, dash, and mechanical work. The dash was recently rebuilt in carbon fiber. "It's popular in race cars," Winkler explains.

The single headlights came from a 1972 Peterbilt in a salvage yard. "The original lights were square. I wanted the look of an old Ford coupe."

Licensed and working, the truck gives a sizzling ride to used trailers and old trucks purchased for resale at Winkler's business. Occasionally he puts it to work in the corn patch on the family farm. In its lifetime, it has rolled across 1.5 million miles. Several times a year it competes at vehicle shows, where the Winklers enjoy showing it off and demonstrating the electronically operated hood and hideaway license plate holder.

"People are fascinated with the 'street rod' look," Winkler says. "A '69 Camaro owner bet me, 'No one comes up to you and says, I had one of them in high school.'" Winkler grins, "I did."

From hood wing to 30-year-old headlamps, this Peterbilt shows off its immaculate attention to detail.

(Above) *The liquid-filled brass gauge, acquired for $20 at a street-rod swap meet, monitors fuel pressure and adds style to the original 359 wood-grain dash.*

(Above Right) *An 8-foot custom-mirrored stainless deck and 6-foot double-door boxes by Taylor Wing add maximum shine. The stacks are 6-inch Dynaflex miter-cut pipes with chromed exhaust from turbo to top. Alcoa polished-aluminum wheels team with 24.5-inch LowPro Firestone rubber.*

(Right) *Larry and Tammy Winkler put years of work into* Barnyard Beast *and now reap the compliments at truck shows.*

(Left) *High-impact color and style routinely draw crowds of admirers who don't have the advantage of an overhead view. This truck wears 50 LED lights.*

BOB AND SHELLEY BRINKER

Grayling, Michigan
Dragon On
Tractor: 2000 Freightliner
  Classic XL
Wheelbase: 265 inches
Engine: 550-horsepower
  Caterpillar 3406E C15
Transmission: 18-speed; 3.73 rears

Trucker stories usually start out, "You won't believe this." This one goes, "Once upon a time, a trucker drove a dragon. . . ."

Bob and Shelley Brinker's fascination with dragons transformed their Freightliner into a fantasy world where dragons rule, knights rescue beautiful maidens from castle dungeons, and wizards maintain a precarious balance between danger and dizzying beauty. Through paint, accessories, and impressive creativity, these Michigan truckers have captured multiple aspects of a wondrous theme and made it their own. Their truck and everything on it are one-of-a-kind.

Spectacular airbrushed murals set the tone against a base of royal metallic plum. Artist Al Proulx, from Sault Ste. Marie, Ontario, worked closely with the Brinkers for two years to develop the art. The front part of the tractor is the dragon's head, and the interior and various painted exterior pieces evoke dungeons, dragons, heroes, and heroines. Dragon scales cover the frame rails from front to back.

On the truck's visor two golden reptilian eyes glow at night. Holes were cut into the visor, filled with clear molded Lexan and glued in, and then

In the wondrous universe Dragon On *occupies, the night is magically lit and a ferocious dragon peers out in search of prey. The 250 or so LED lights are by Truck-Lite. A dazzling 24-inch chrome bumper from Valley Chrome Plating features 24 LEDs alone, not counting the light box behind the laser-cut name.*

the eye details were painted on. Lights behind the visor bring them to life. It's as if a dragon were actually glowering back at onlookers.

Lifting the hood reveals a surprise: the engine is painted like the American flag in red, white, and blue. "This was the only place we could show our appreciation to U.S. troops," Bob explains. "My dad and hers, our nephew, and son were in the army, but this is for everyone in the U.S. Armed Forces."

For all its magical beauty, *Dragon On* is a working truck that transports lumber and steel on a 48-foot flatbed to home-improvement centers and job sites throughout the I-65 and I-75 corridors. Bob recalls taking a load of lumber to a remote dam site 14 miles into a national forest in the Upper Peninsula of Michigan. He had just been to a show and the truck was polished to the max, and there he sat in mud almost covering the axles. Then he had to back out the same narrow, rutted road he took in. As those in the biz like to say, "That's truckin'."

Bob has been driving since 1981 and has covered 578,680 miles in *Dragon On*. He has been with Ken Graham Trucking for 15 years, the last five as an owner-operator.

Shelley, a full-time sergeant first class in the Michigan Army National Guard, also holds a commercial driver's license (CDL) and its military equivalent. She is responsible for logistics at Camp Grayling. Shelley was a co-driver for 10 years.

For truck shows, Shelley takes leave from duty to help her husband. They dress in costume: he's a wizard, she's a princess, and the truck is enormously popular. As members of the National Association of Show Trucks (NAST), the couple won the 2003 Truck-Lite Trophy Championship series and bested their peers in a series of nationwide competitions.

(Below) Enter the dungeon—the 70-inch condo-style cab and sleeper with dragon seat covers and oak doors throughout. The walls, dash, and headliner are airbrushed to emulate stone. Purple jewels tip all switch extensions. The beds are covered with dragoned purple throws. Skulls and chains accessorize the dash and bunk.

(Above) Princess Shelley and Royal Wizard Bob Brinker show off their dragon diesel. The knight on the hood is painted with a special 3-D technique. Above the knight, hidden in a red cloud, is a ghosted dragon outlined in white pearl. The sun has to hit the image in just the right way for the dragon to appear. Fuel tank straps were etched by artist Jim Shively. Tires are 24.5 Goodyear low-profiles glitzed up with Accuride Accu-shield no-polish aluminum rims.

(Opposite) Dragons are everywhere, including here on the rear fender, which was made by WTI. Behind it, another pair of dragon's eyes peers from a lair painted on the lighted aluminum headache rack. Although you can't see her, a drop-dead-gorgeous princess is painted above the rack. She is holding a steely dragon on a chain leash.

DON AND SUSAN PARDUE

Clarksville, Georgia
Bad to the Bone
Tractor: 2002 Peterbilt 379
  extended hood
Wheelbase: 365 inches
Engine: 600-horsepower Caterpillar C16
Transmission: 18-speed; 3.55 rears

Some truckers are never satisfied with the status quo. They keep reinventing their wheels and challenging themselves to come up with a new look that will satisfy the itch to drive something that looks nothing like anyone else has. Don and Susan Pardue's *Bad to the Bone* was a splendid looking truck. That was then, this is now, and now the truck looks entirely different and even more splendid than before. "This is the third incarnation of the truck," Don says. "It's pretty drastic. I'm trying to make it better and different."

The Pardues, the truck's owner-operators, had placed in truck shows with earlier versions, but with version number three they are in hot pursuit of a Best of Show award. "We haven't chromed every piece of metal. There's no stainless under the hood or fenders. Nothing here has to be removed [after a show] to return to work," he says.

The tractor is dark blue metallic and is accented with 342 LED lights by Trux, plus flames, murals, and bold magenta stripes and fenders marbleized in a radical technique perfected by painter Jay Griffin at the K & L Chrome Shop, where the work was done. "The effect is kind of translucent, like a bowling ball," Pardue quips.

The awesome front bumper carries a double row of clear-lensed LEDs, a whopping 108 inches all, with the truck's name laser-cut into the bumper and backlit. Custom-painted murals and flames were done by Jay Griffin at the K & L Chrome Shop in Florence, South Carolina. Stainless toolboxes by Taylor Wing store their flatbed gear.

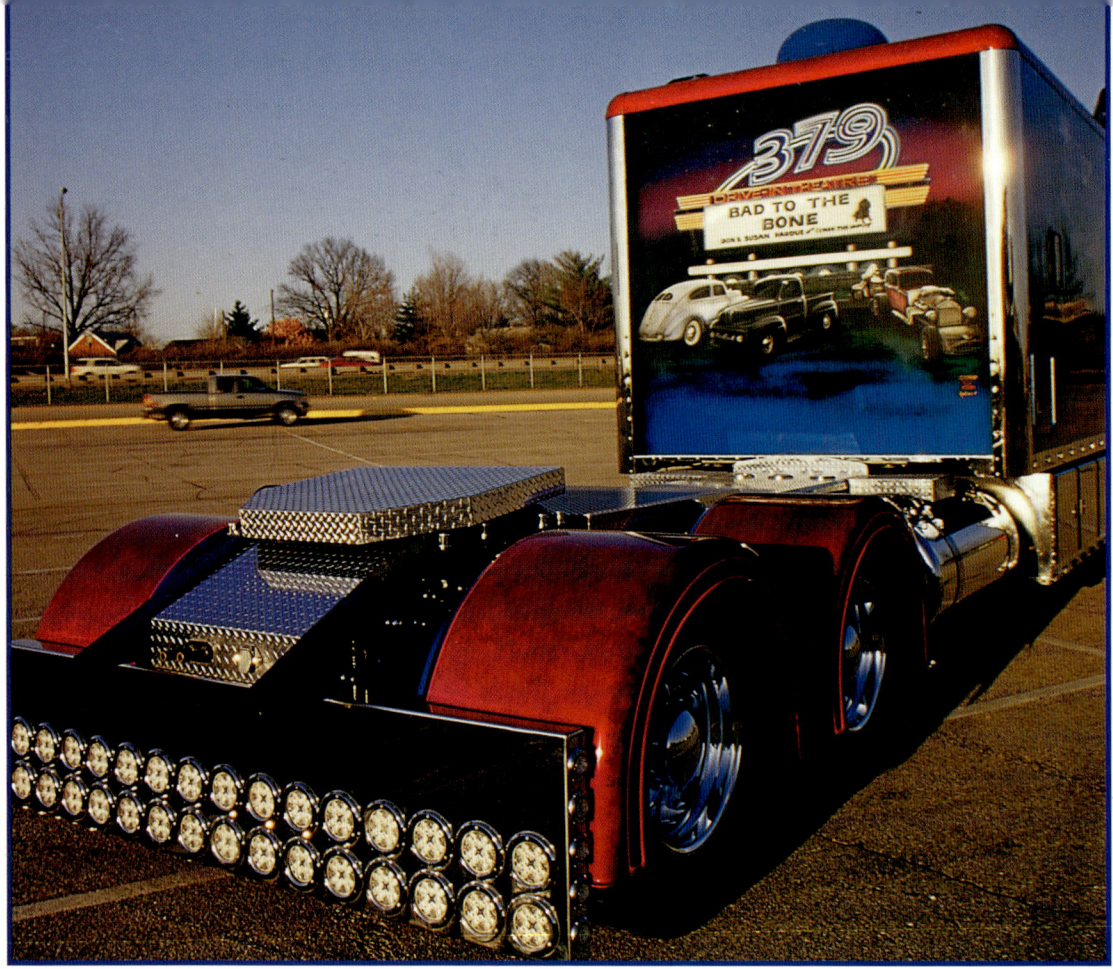

The stainless-steel back bumper is dressed to impress with a double row of clear-lensed LEDs. The movie-theater theme continues on the sleeper's back wall with a lineup of antique vehicles. Note the rich color and texture in the fender's paint.

The murals on three sides, also by Griffin, celebrate the age of drive-ins, both diners and movies, and honor family and friends. The passenger-side mural depicts a drive-in theater packed with cool street rods from the 1950s. On the back wall, a "379" marquee is the destination for a 1952 Ford pickup, a 1944 Deluxe owned by Don's uncle, a 1931 Ford Bantam that belonged to the friend who taught Don to drive, and the couple's own Honda Valkyrie trike. The driver's side mural features "Humdinger," an old-time truck-stop diner named after one that Don's dad operated years ago. Old fuel pumps and old trucks are also included. "There's a lot of family history in the picture," Susan says.

The total weight of the tractor alone, which shoulders a 150-inch ARI-built bunk, is 30,000 pounds fully loaded with fuel and water. They carry 44 gallons for the shower and dishes, plus a 5-gallon potable water reservoir filled with water from home.

Don emphasizes that this is a work truck with close to half a million miles on it. The couple specializes in transporting military equipment, assorted vehicles, and personnel carriers to armed service bases throughout the country. They pull a removable-gooseneck (RGN) trailer that comes apart and allows vehicles to be driven directly onto and off the trailer.

The Pardues have been in the truck business for 21 years and with their present carrier for 12. Both of them drive. "Everything we do requires team operations in order to serve our customer, which is the U.S. government," Don says. The high level of interior comfort is a work necessity as this type of operation is constantly moving, with few opportunities for layovers.

Pardue fell into trucking quite accidentally. After serving in Korea, he enrolled in a dental college and got a part-time job driving a truck. "I got the bug. I liked the traveling. A family friend taught me to drive and I bought a truck. I've been doing it ever since."

Married in 1973, the couple found themselves at a juncture. "Sue got tired of me being gone. It was either get in the truck with me and learn to drive it, or go the other way. She got on board." It's her woman's touch that imbues the spacious bunk with homestyle comfort. Their toy poodle, Conan, their "black-furred kid," has been with them for 9 years.

Decorated with 1950s memorabilia, this well-equipped sleeper has all the comforts of home, including a separate bathroom with standup shower, 54-inch bunk, two swing-out tables (one doubles as a nightstand), full-size refrigerator/freezer, extra-deep sink with separate water spigot, and a microwave/convection oven. Rope lighting serves as a night-light.

In front of their beautifully custom-painted hood, Don and his wife, Susan, show off their 1950s outfits they donned on judging day at the Paul K. Young Memorial Truck Beauty Championships in Louisville, Kentucky, in 2005.

JONATHAN HUNSICKER JR.

Dover, Pennsylvania
Double Trouble
Tractor: 2000 Mack Vision
Wheelbase: 234 inches
Engine: 460-horsepower Mack
Transmission: Eaton 13-speed;
   3.7 rears

You have to love the color on this Mack Vision: mulberry mica zapped with gold trim. The addition of light pearl metallic to the paint allows the color to shift in the sun, romping from pink to maroon to purple. The owner of this eye-catching 100-year-anniversary model readily admits the cheery berry hue grew on him. "I love the color now. It took some time to come up with the accent colors, though," Jonathan Hunsicker admits.

Hunsicker worked with local painter George Williamson from GW Signs and settled on magenta pink for the spirited pinstriping and contrast striping in four different shades of teal blue. All the paint work, including the lettering, was done by hand. The unusual combination, teamed with distinctive anodized gold metal accents, makes for a truck that turns heads and draws nods of approval. A Bulldog this pretty is a rare sight; it draws as many compliments as a cute puppy. "People can't believe somebody would put that much work into a truck," the proud owner says.

Although the anniversary model was released in black with gold trim, this particular tractor was specially painted for its debut at the renowned Mid-America Trucking Show in 2000.

Hunsicker saw it, liked it, and, as he said, "The price was right." He bought it right off the show floor.

Two generations of Hunsicker men have driven Mack trucks before Jonathan. His father's company ran nothing but Mack trucks. After completing Mack mechanic training at "Mack University" in Allentown, Pennsylvania, Hunsicker launched his own trucking career. He hit the road in 1989, and in 1996 he became an owner-operator. This truck, his third, was purchased in 2000.

Stylized vinyl bulldogs personalize the truck even more. The dogs on the roof are named for the truck's owner; his wife, Michelle; and their daughter, Sarah. There are also two dogs on each side of the truck. "It's a tradition my dad, Tim, started on his trucks, only he used stars with our family's names on them. I wanted to do that, too, and this is my way to carry it on," Hunsicker says.

Inside the cab is stock, spec'd with Mack's extra-wide, extra-tall swivel seats embroidered with the 100-year emblem on the back support. This Bulldog has run over 250,000 miles and is currently pulling a 42-foot dry-bulk tanker of cement powder in the Northeast.

LACEY DALTON

L.A. Dalton Systems
Caledonia, Ontario, Canada
Blood, Sweat, and 30 Years
Tractor: 2004 Peterbilt 379
Wheelbase: 325 inches
Engine: 475-horsepower
  Caterpillar
Transmission: Meritor 12-speed
  automatic; 3.55 rears
Trailer: 2004 48-foot East
  flatbed R-axle

It has been 30 years since he bought his first truck, and Lacey Dalton is still following the white line. Actually, he has been trucking for a total of 42 years and says he always knew it was what he was meant to do. He bought his first truck in 1975 and has been an owner-operator for 30 years, hence the truck's name: *Blood, Sweat, and 30 Years*.

Dalton calls himself "truck crazy." Just look at this outfit, the culmination of years of accumulating ideas as he drove interstates in the United States and Canada. Nobody but Dalton has ideas like these, so take notes.

Blood, Sweat, and 30 Years is one long sweep of beauty on 14 wheels. Tires are single Michelin X-Ones. The body on the back is enclosed in a lighted custom box, which is what you'd expect to see on a tow rig, but only sexier. There are no fenders or back bumper. "I wanted everything filled in," Dalton says.

Hawaiian orchid and royal blue stripes jazz up the black body. The rivetless visor is 1 inch longer than standard. Doors have been suicided and the diamond-shaped LEDs on the air cleaners are motorcycle taillights. The 48-foot East flatbed has a 10-1 spread in back and two custom-made 9-foot lifts. The tractor bumper is 18 inches deep, and the stainless grille bars, headlight rings, and battery-box covers are all custom.

Stainless panels with mitered breaks, like pleating, add definition to the doors. All of the stainless work was done in-house by Louie Poirier. Cherrywood borders accent the stainless. The two-tone gray leather seats came from a Peterbilt 379X. The dash is covered in carbon fiber and the overhead console is leather. The NASCAR steering wheel lifts off. "It's quick release for security. If you can't steer it, you can't steal it," Dalton says.

The meticulous pinstriping was done by hand, the sparkly clear-coat paint was custom mixed with metallics, and the frame was painstakingly polished out. Diamond-shaped LEDs on air cleaners are part of the 216 lights overall. Inside, stainless panels with mitered breaks that appear pleated sparkle on doors and walls. Floors are tiled in two colors of onyx-looking ceramic.

This is Dalton's flagship to his fleet made up of 36 steel haulers and several owner-operators. Steel coils and slabs going to automotive plants ride the trailers. Long hauls are made mostly to Ohio, Alabama, and Tennessee. "When I meet a new customer, this truck is a great ice breaker," Dalton says. "Everybody looks it over. But that's not always a good thing. It can drive you crazy in a good way.

Drivers run alongside me, checking out the details, wandering into my lane. In truck stops it's a great attention getter."

It took more than two years' worth of work to bring the 75-foot-long truck to this point. The look Dalton was striving for was a show truck of the mid-1980s, when rigs with matching tractor and trailer were more popular than they are now. "They used less stainless then and paint was a more important component to tie the two together than it is now," Dalton explains. Dalton's entire trailer is polished out, which was a job that took months, but look at the results. What shine!

Another detail that sets this truck apart is its use of 11x22.5 Michelin X-Ones (single tires) on both pieces of equipment. Front tires and rims are designed for

Inside the 150-inch American Reliance Industries (ARI) sleeper, Dalton created a luxurious haven with ceramic onyx-tiled floor and stainless and mirror panels on walls, cabinets, and closets. A futon bed is visible, but the upper bunk is hidden. The ceiling is mirrored and lined with blue glow wire. More luxe details are the Corian counters and deep luster cherrywood cabinets with brass trims. There's a shower/toilet, microwave, and hot plate. The built-in flat-screen TV has "follow-me" satellite TV tracking.

a Prevos bus and are rated at 15,000 pounds. Wheels are the Alcoa Dura-Brites that never need polishing.

He carries three 100-gallon water tanks: two on the tractor and one on the trailer. One on the tractor serves the shower and sink, and the other holds gray water. Both tanks on the tractor are hidden by the frame enclosure. The trailer tank holds deionized water. He hooks it to a pressure washer and uses it to give the rig a spot-free rinse at shows.

Look at the magnificent detailing on this box surround Dalton had custom built to take the place of bumper and fenders. It hides the tractor's two 100-gallon water tanks. All of the bolts are hidden. Most of the lights on the overall rig are by Panelite.

OWNER: MIKE MCLANE
DRIVER: MAX HAERTLING

Popular Bluff, Missouri
Mad Max
Tractor: 1997 Kenworth
   W900L Studio
Wheelbase: 298 inches
Engine: 600-horsepower
   Caterpillar 3406E
Transmission: RTX 2018B
   18-speed; Eaton 48,000-pound
   rears 3.55 ratio
Trailer: 1998 50-foot Great Dane
   ThermaCube reefer

Everything about *Mad Max* points to owner Mike McLane's obsession with trucks. "I'm just kind of a truck fanatic in general," says this smiling lifelong trucker. "I enjoy looking at other guys' equipment as much as they like looking at mine." *Mad Max* makes a weekly run to California or the Northwest transporting furniture, cheese, and heating and air-conditioner parts. Backhauls of apples, potatoes, and other fresh produce come back east to Tennessee, Kentucky, and Missouri.

Drivers react to the glorious rig with big smiles and thumbs-up as they pass by. Whether it's McLane behind the wheel or Max Haertling, the truck's dedicated road driver, the gratitude for all the attention is humbly received and happily acknowledged. "Max enjoys the drivers' hollering at

The 22-inch boltless stainless-steel bumpers are by Rigskirts, which also made the three tool boxes, the battery box, and the stainless fairings on the dual 150-gallon tanks. Among the 280 truck and trailer LED lights are new cab and sleeper clearance lights with 36 diodes in each light. Eight-inch stacks wear turnout tops from 4 State Trucks. The trailer door trim is painted to contrast with the blazingly bright stainless. The wheels are by Alcoa and tires are by Bridgestone.

88

That's Mike McLane atop the engine and Max Haertling below, preparing Mad Max *for a truck show. The engine is dressed in stainless trim and filter wraps by Rigskirts, plus stainless on the fan shroud, shocks, and leaf springs. The combo's brake chambers are covered with reconfigured hubcaps. Max and Mike added stainless backing plates on the brakes themselves.*

him better than winning a trophy," says McLane. "You can tell it blows him up big time. And he always says 'Thanks.'"

That said, the truck has earned a whopping 36 trophies in the two years it's been competing in truck shows.

Mad Max deserves maximum attention for its old-style Kenworth Seminole paint design in striking Viper red and glazed white, plus the highly polished trim, custom stainless accents, and 280 LED lights.

Stainless lovers find much to admire on this truck. Original headlights were replaced by Double JJ brackets with stainless reproduction lights from 4 State Trucks. A custom grille gives a narrow look to the hood. The massive bumper is a boltless 22-inch Texas square. The stainless trailer doors are mirror-polished and the entire interior floor (cab and bunk) is polished stainless set off with rosewood accent pieces.

"All my nice stainless is by Rigskirts or [Max and I] made it ourselves," McLane notes. "Max and I polished the doors and all the trim by machine, and then hand polished both rails, too. It took us awhile. When we first showed it, Vlad [Vladimir Bilik, well-known show trucker] came over to me and said 'Nobody ever does the top rail!' He noticed it immediately," McLane says with obvious pride.

Noteworthy design elements include the cool custom hood by Truk-Rodz. "We lengthened the front fenders so it looks like the truck's been lowered and it fills up space between the front tire and fender," McLane explains. He liked the hood so much that he had one built for another of his trucks.

McLane was 14 years old when he started working around trucks. Later he hauled cattle. "We had so many trucks, we built a shop in 1977 and we live 300 yards behind it. There's a small shop just for *Mad Max.*"

McLane has owned a dozen trucks but sold them in 1992 to join his dad in McLane Transport, the family business. Today their fleet numbers about 115 reefer trailers and 60 tractors, plus a handful of leased operators. In what is truly an American dream, the business is run by his parents, J. P. and Mary McLane, sister Becky Brooks, and her husband, Alan. His oldest boy, Lance, works in the shop and his wife, Beth, works in the office.

This stainless-steel interior flooring is a rare sight. It was made by Rigskirts and was originally a prototype for Kenworth. Max and Mike measured the floor, had Rigskirts make it, and the two of them installed the flooring. Non-slip bathroom rugs protect the surface. The seats are Bostrom Wide Glide Low Riders. Rosewood trims and accessories are used throughout the interior. Every switch and screw in the dash is jeweled in red.

MONT BOARDMAN

Magna, Utah
Barbedwire & Roses
Tractor: 2004 Peterbilt 379
   short hood
Wheelbase: 252 inches
Engine: 550-horsepower
   Caterpillar C15
Transmission: Eaton 13-speed;
   3.25 rears
Trailer: 2004 Cottrell C7512
   car hauler

Certain trucks sparkle with creativity from every angle, and this is a wonderful example. Front to back, the spectacular red and stainless-steel-clad car hauler stands up and shouts custom.

Mont Boardman came to this specialized hauling niche by accident. He was a 22-year-old truck mechanic with part-time road experience when he spotted an ad from an auto transporter. He signed on, and in about six weeks he learned the basics of tying down cars and getting them on and off the truck. It took another six months for him to get comfortable with his job.

That was five years ago, and this is his second truck, his first new one. Operating under lease to Spider Auto Transport, Inc., he carries cars from auctions and car rental companies to auto dealerships, mostly west of the Mississippi. Boardman has put 184,803 miles on the truck since its purchase and runs solo.

Boardman's Viper red and platinum Peterbilt wears a 16-inch Texas square bumper by Valley Chrome Plating. Bumper lighting includes six marker/turn-signal lights and eight round Spyder lights by Grand General. The visor is 10 inches of stainless steel. Boardman uses Michelin 22.5s teamed with Alcoa polished-aluminum rims. The red bug screen complements the stainless and costs little to achieve a great look. Note the Cadillac medallions on the hood.

93

All 279 lights, including markers, are clear-lens Spyder LEDs by Grand General. "I think they blend right in with the stainless and just bring it altogether," he explains.

The spidery graphics by Raven of Winter Garden, Florida, were inspired by the name of Boardman's lease carrier. "I wanted to have fun with [the theme], do it kinda wild, but keep it neat," Boardman says. He put a twist on the look of old-school round headlights by mounting high-intensity Xenon lamps into Double JJ brackets. The Peterbilt hood emblems are sparkly red inside, outlined in chrome, with the word Cadillac in the middle. Boardman credits a dispatcher with the idea: "He was checking out the truck and he told me, 'It's not a truck anymore. It's like driving a Cadillac,' and it kinda stuck."

Stainless is the third color on this outfit. The impact is particularly impressive on the trailer where light-studded panels adorn almost every open surface. T & C Welding of Jacksonville, Florida, did the work and custom built the tractor's head rack, which holds three cars—one on the roof, one behind the cab, and one stacked on top of the one behind the cab.

The same approach to customization is evident inside the cab and 48-inch stock sleeper, which was ordered with a sliding rear window. Boardman made a polished aluminum shelf to hold his 15-inch LCD television. A Sony PlayStation 2 doubles as a DVD player. A custom-made speaker box under the bunk holds three 10-inch competition subwoofers powered by a 1,800-watt amplifier.

Boardman's wife, Carolynn, used red velvet to make curtains, pillows, a dash mat, and a gear-shifter boot. An auxiliary Webasto diesel-burning heater keeps the bunk toasty in the winter. Red leather Wide Ride Bostrom seats are in tune with the red interior. "It's my home away from home," Mont says, "I want it to be nice."

The dash carries the full gauge package, including the Caterpillar I.D. system. The sound system is an Alpine stereo/CD player with XM satellite radio. All toggle-switch extensions are tipped with red jewels. The stock steering wheel has been upgraded to a stainless-and-rosewood model. Metal makes an impact with chrome steering-column covers, and stainless-steel pedals, door handles, and arm rests. "I was going for the shine. I love chrome," Boardman explains.

Spider Auto Transport, Inc., inspires the spider-web motif on Boardman's truck. The second design is Barbedwire and Roses, with the legend scripted across the back of the bunk and shown here in a graphic below the door. During shows, Boardman displays a crystal globe on the hood where a traditional ornament would otherwise be found. Inside the globe is a red rose, and the base is circled with barbed wire.

(Right) Boardman's headlights draw raves from fellow drivers when he flashes clearance signals. "They go crazy over them," he notes. He loves the look of the lights as well as their performance. "They shine out farther without blinding others, light up lines better at night and on wet roads, and they work better in fog."

Index